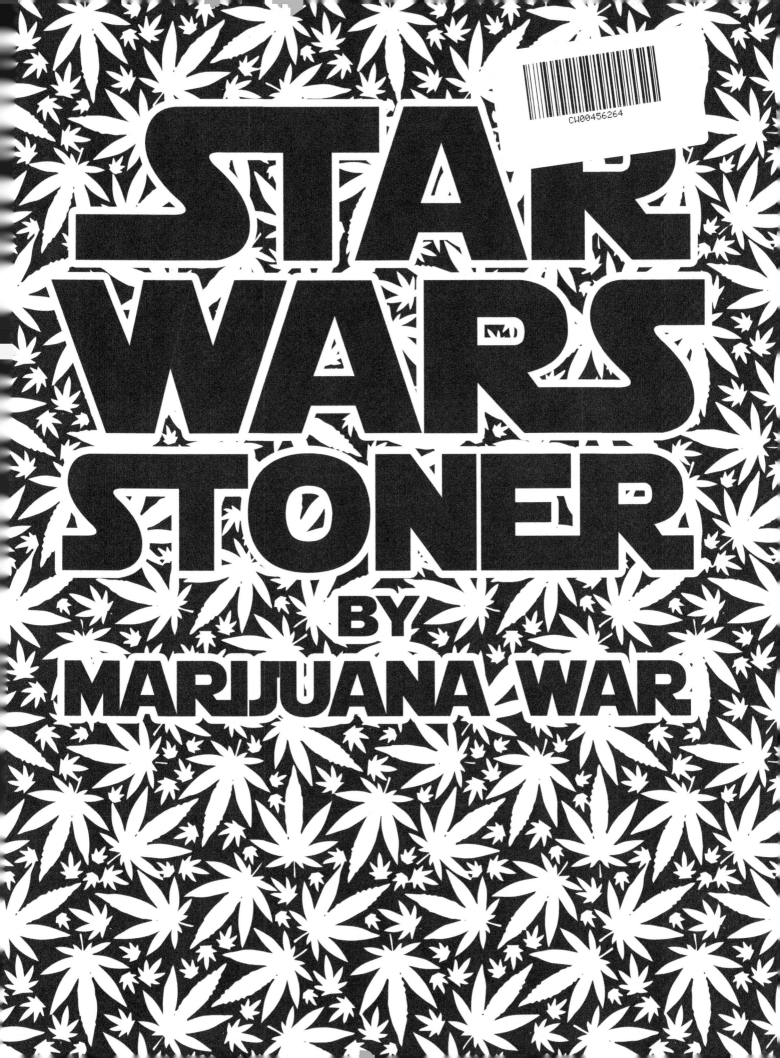

STAR WARS STONER

BY

MARIJUANA WAR

TEST COLOR PAGE

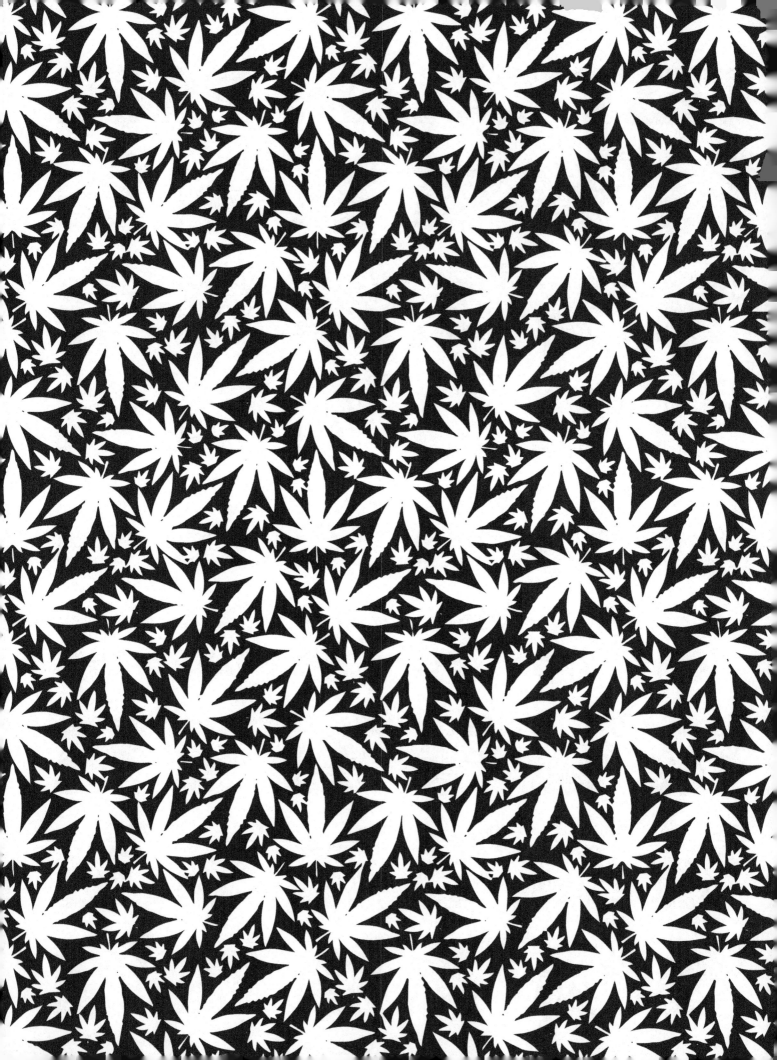

TEST COLOR PAGE

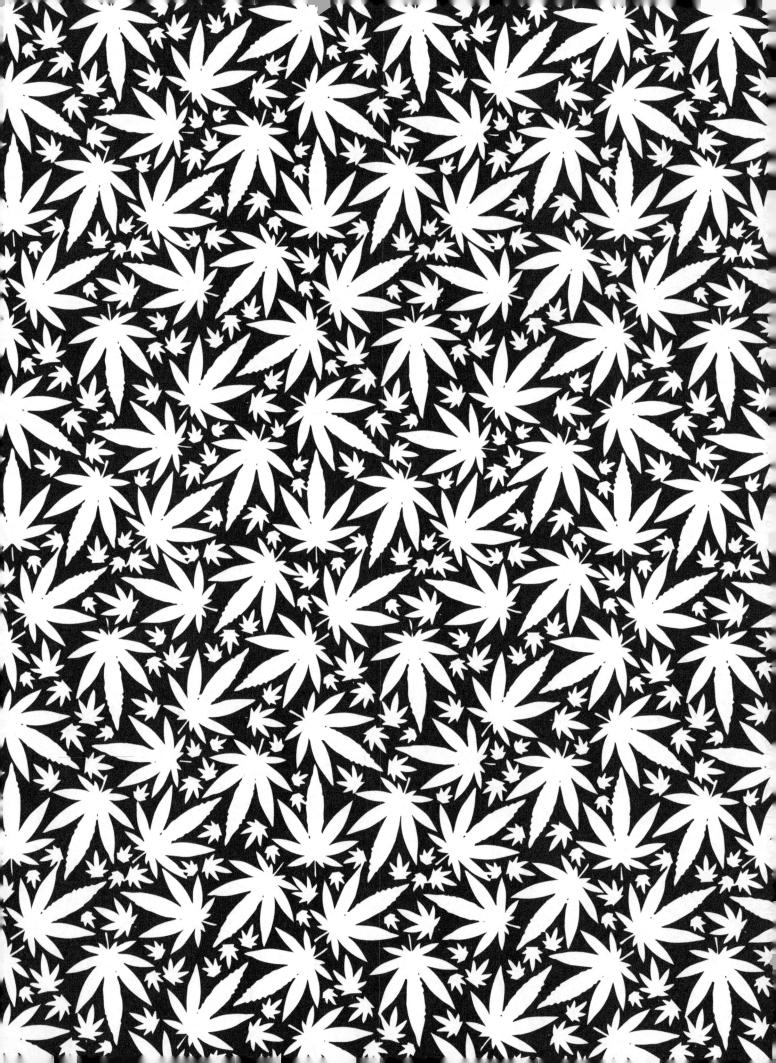

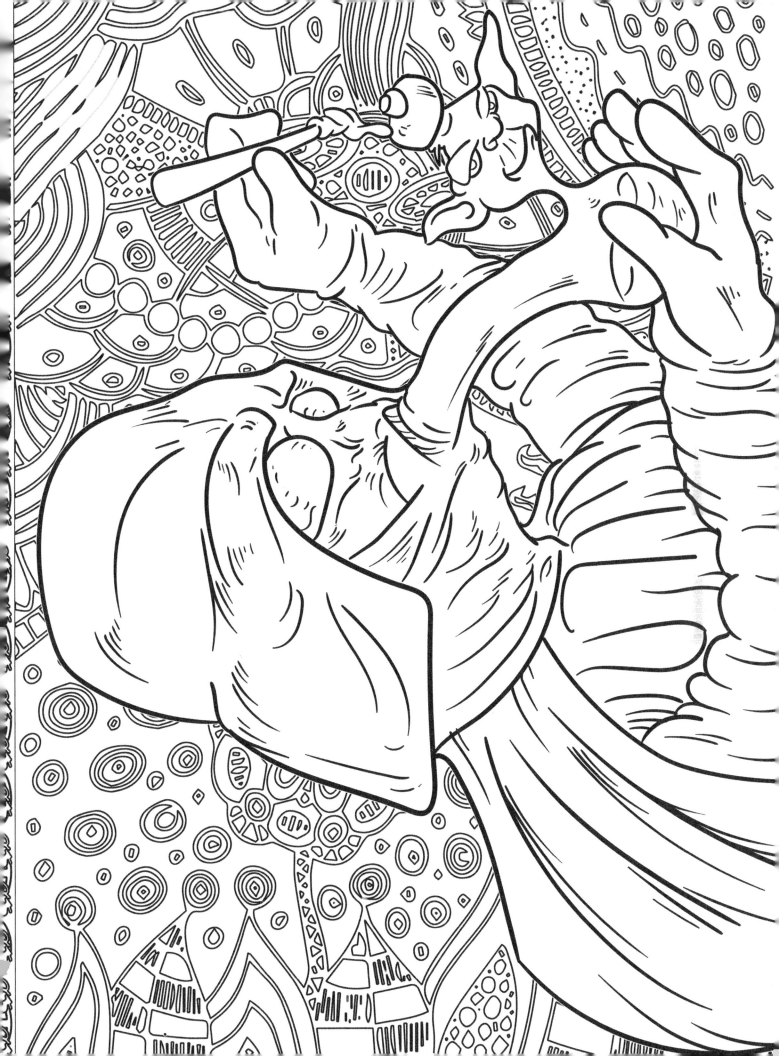

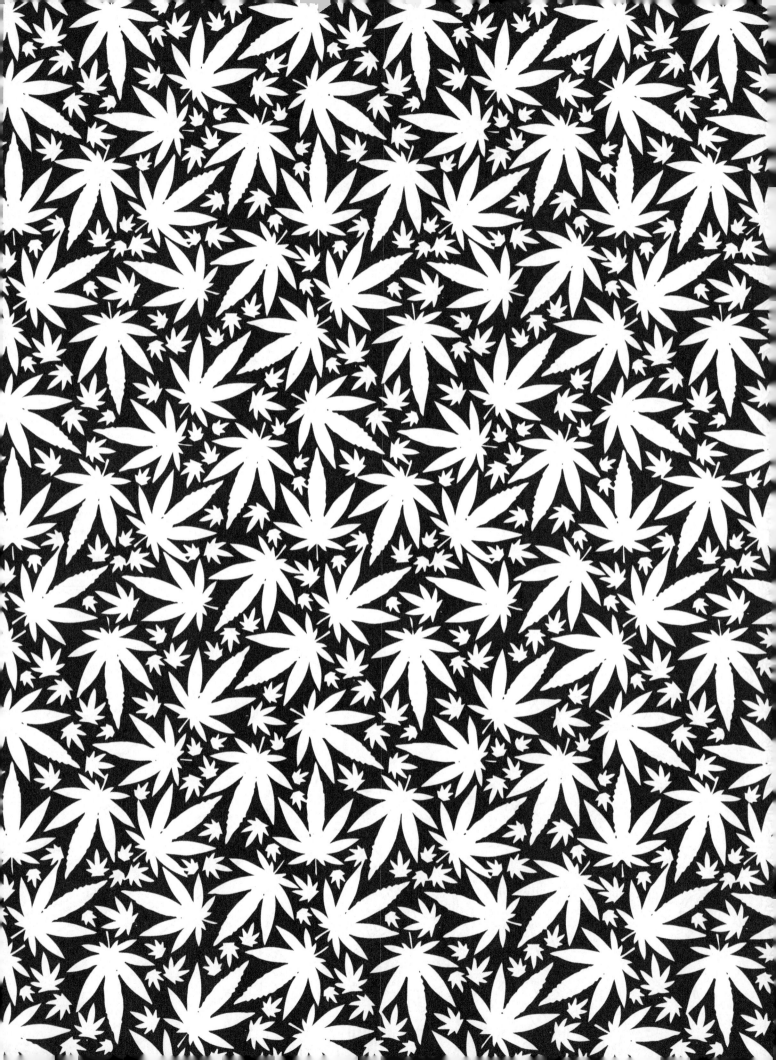

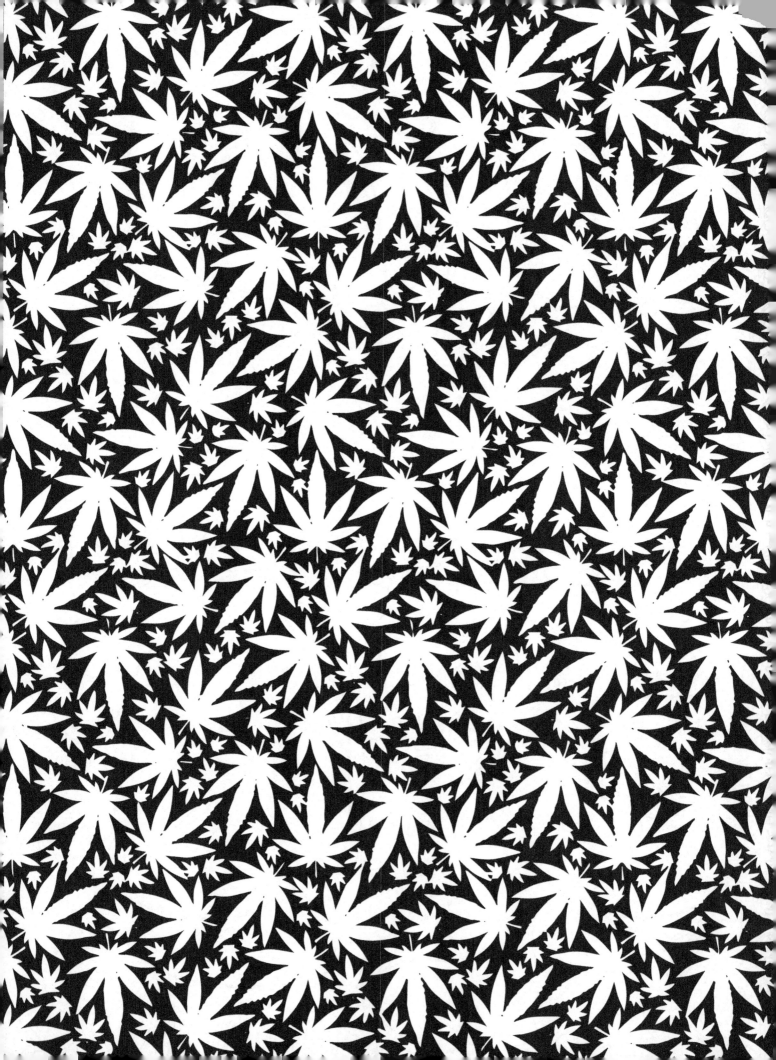

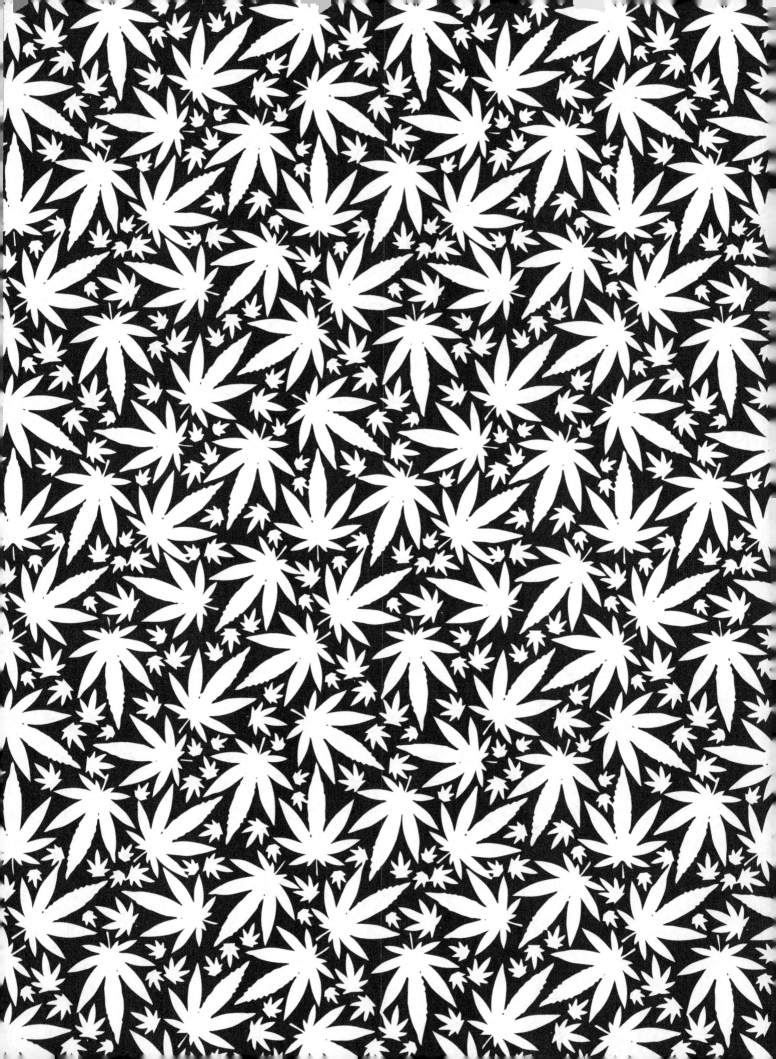

DEAR OUR BELOVED CUSTOMERS,

HT'S A GREAT HONOR FOR US TO SERVE YOU

AND WE WOULD LIKE TO THANK YOU FOR CHOOSING OUR PRODUCTS.

SO IF THIS BOOK BRINGS YOU HAPPINESS AND ENJOYMENT

COULD YOU PLEASE SHARE YOU WONDERFUL EXPERIENCE ON AMAZON.

THAT WOULD BE THE BIGGEST MOTIVATION FOR US TO DEVELOP DAY BY DAY.

THANKS SO MUCH AND WISH YOU BEST LUCK!

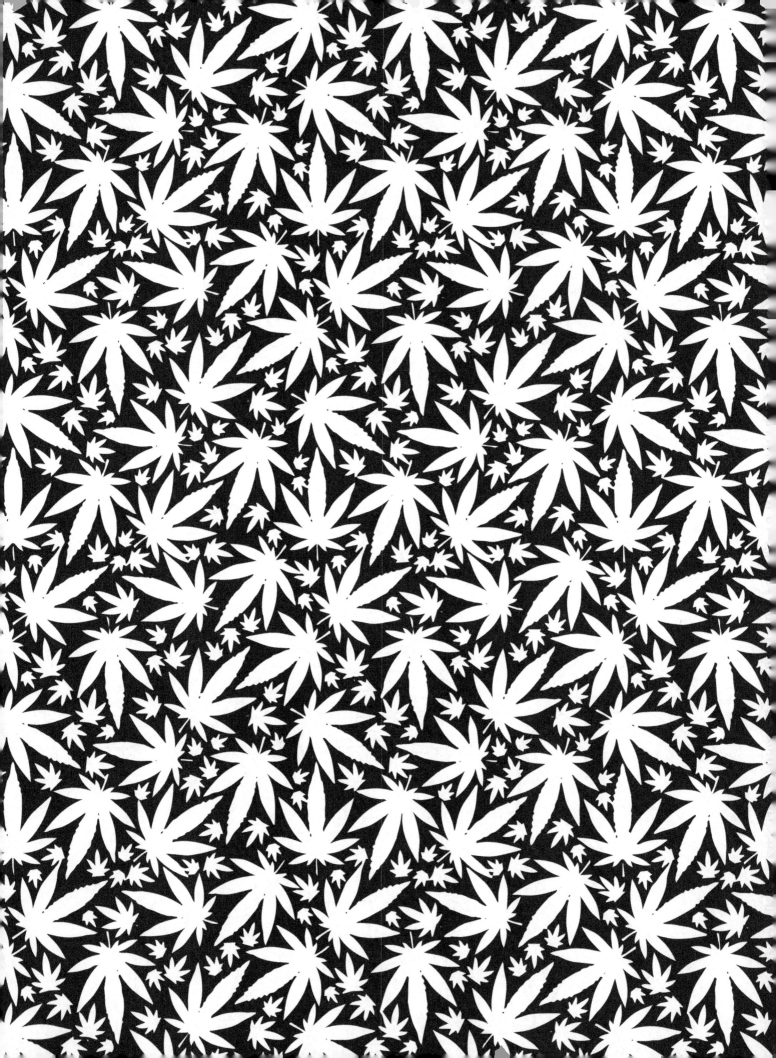

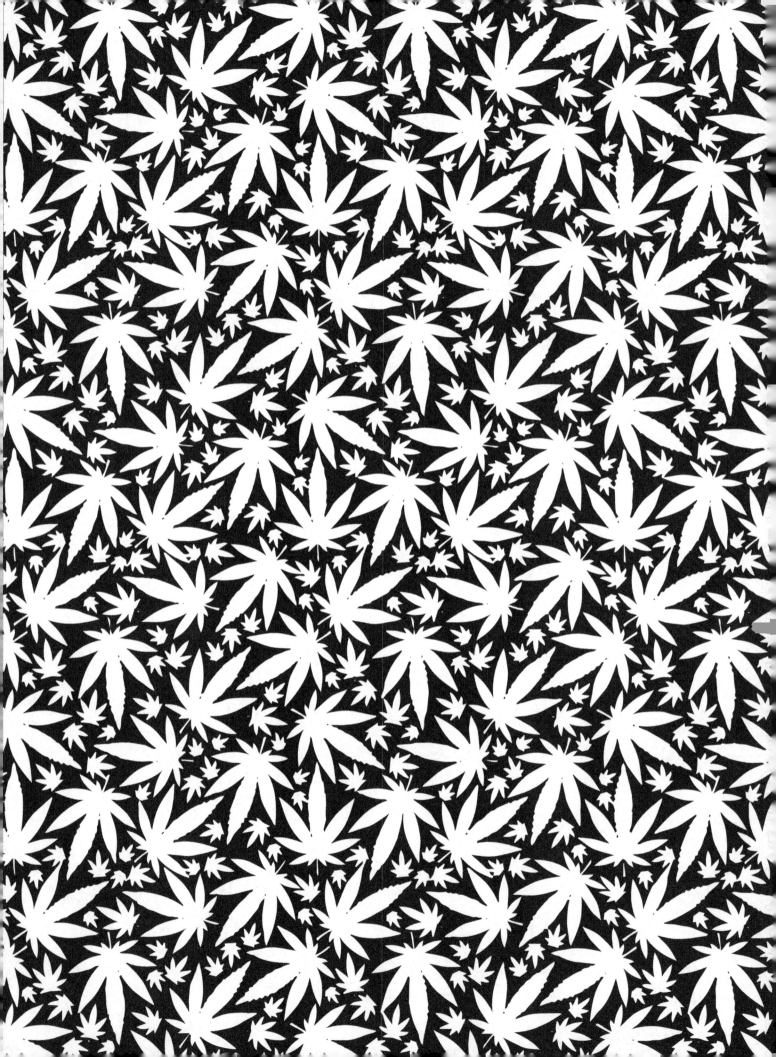

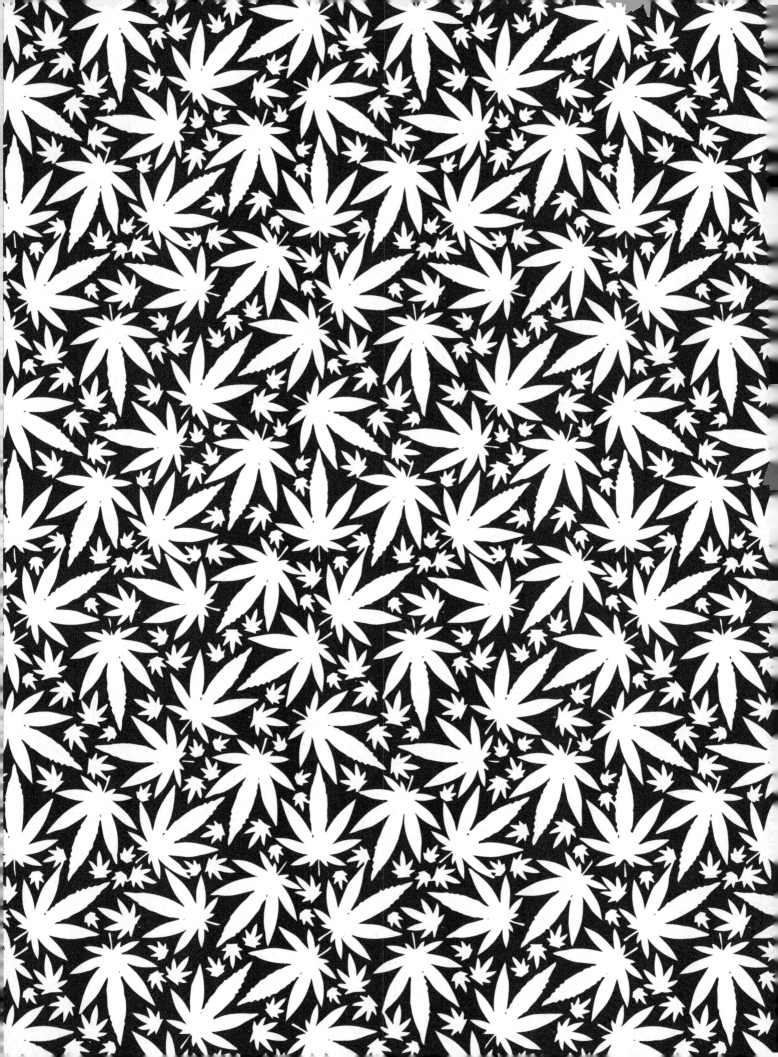

Printed in Great Britain
by Amazon